God's Amazing Normal

The joy of new life in Christ

I dream about seeing God's children mature and have the joy of birthing others into a new life in Christ! Not only is this Christ's command and one of the most exhilarating experiences in life, but it is also God's amazing and fulfilling normal.

Larry

Larry DeWitt

xulon
PRESS

Table of Contents

—⟋⟍—

Chapter   Page

Acknowledgments

—⋙—

My gratitude to Christ . . .

for rescuing me, allowing me to serve Him, and giving me a great hope;

for my lovely lady, Beccy, for 50 years of loving and serving Christ together. She encouraged me—almost forever—to put my heart in writing and has offered practical insights in preparing this for you;

for Bette Holzer, my ministry assistant, who has worked with me every step of the way from the beginning through the final editing of this book;

for Bill Myers, recognized prolific Christian writer, who has shepherded me and assumed the role of editor to help me bring vitality to these concepts;

for people from Calvary Community Church, who I've pastored, and who have learned to live a fruitful pray-care-share lifestyle; and

for Mission America Coalition and its president, Paul Cedar, who has opened the door for me, as national facilitator for pastors, to take these concepts to pastors and leaders in cities throughout the nation.

In Christ's incredible name,

Larry DeWitt

Endorsements

—‿ɷ‿—

My friendship with Larry DeWitt began in the mid 1980s when both of us were serving as pastors in Southern California. Larry was the founder and pastor of a large, fast-growing church in Southern California. The major thrust of Larry DeWitt's ministry was to be pastor—that was his heart and passion. He loved people. He saw himself as called by God to care for the flock that He has entrusted to his care. Although he was effective in other areas of ministry, his highest priority was to pastor the congregation of Calvary Community Church. And he did it extremely well.

Larry invited me to preach at Calvary Church about the Lighthouse Movement, which encouraged Christians to adopt a lifestyle of prayer-care-share. They invited Christ followers at Calvary to pray for family members and friends who were not followers of Jesus, to care for them—authentically love them in every possible way—and to share with them lovingly and appropriately the good news of the gospel.

Larry and his church responded in an incredible way. Although thousands of churches were involved in the Lighthouse

Movement, Calvary Community Church became the largest and perhaps the most effective in the entire nation.

A few years later, Larry retired from his pastorate and formed the Cornerstone Network. Within that context, he served on the Facilitation Team of the Mission America Coalition as our national facilitator of pastoral ministries. The Lord used him wonderfully to minister to pastors across the nation. As a part of that pastoral ministry, he has had a significant ministry within the "Loving our Communities to Christ" initiative of the Mission America Coalition/U.S. Lausanne Committee.

Larry DeWitt is one of the most effective pastors I have ever known. It has been a great joy to partner in ministry with him. I am so grateful that he has written this book. He is uniquely quali-fied and prepared to do so. I highly commend this exceptional pastor and this excellent book to you.

Dr. Paul Cedar

Chairman, The Mission America Coalition

# # # # #

God's Amazing Normal is a crisp distillation of decades of pastoring . . . boiled down to a crystal clear model of ministry. Over the past 35+ years (as a consultant), I have watched over 200 pastors/churches very close-up. Larry DeWitt and the pray-care-share model of ministry is as real—and as effective—as it gets. This book is a classic . . . keep your first edition!

Bob Biehl

Executive Mentor

# # # # #

Are you a follower of Jesus needing encouragement, a discipler among friends, a spiritual parent with a heart of adoption toward others? This is your book. *God's Amazing Normal* is a great story, great teaching, and an inspiring practical guide.

John Dawson

International Convener - President Emeritus, Youth With A Mission

# # # # #

Well done, Larry! You have done a great job of communicating huge truths in a very readable, practical, attractive, brief manner. What a great story! You have demonstrated that "the main thing is always keep the main thing the main thing!"

Many other spiritual leaders will read this book and become more convinced and equipped to be successful at convincing the "average person in the pew" that they can be involved in God's great mission here on earth.

Dennis Fuqua

President, International Renewal Ministries (www.prayer-summits.net)

# # # # #

God's Amazing Normal is authored from the life of what may be America's premier pray-care-share pastor! My friend and colleague Larry DeWitt casts a Christ-centered vision for congregations of believers who live the lifestyle of interceding for lost persons, loving the least as well as those who lead, and explaining the gospel in clear and compelling ways to their neighbors.

Be careful! The many stories you'll encounter are able to do more than inspire you. Listen to them in a way that allows you to first implement the principles into your own life so that you begin to live the lifestyle he so clearly defines and describes. Then, look for ways to invite those in the stewardship of your ministry to take this praying-caring-sharing journey with you. Your family. A small group. Maybe an entire congregation . . . or even, a collaboration of congregations who are ready to love their communities to Christ. *God's Amazing Normal* will then become more than a message and a book of motivating stories; it will explode with insights and ideas of how to equip others to explore a Christ-centered lifestyle.

Pastor Larry is our guide and our teacher because he has truly been there and done that. Many more of us will be able to say the same once we have begun to walk with the Christ of our faith, hope, and love he so often and so clearly points us to in this book.

Phil Miglioratti
Founder, National Pastors' Prayer Network
Mission America Coalition / Loving Our Communities to Christ

# # # # #

Larry DeWitt's ministry is not only Christ focused but practical in its application. I love to get Larry around young pastors and let him fill them with enthusiasm and passion for the living Christ—the only One who can change lives. In the book *God's Amazing Normal*, you feel Larry's heart for his theme, "Make much of Jesus," and hear about practical and time-tested ways to bring Christ to people and people to Christ. I wholeheartedly endorse reading his book.

Bill Hossler

President, Missionary Church, Inc.

# # # # #

I believe there is a "Prayer, Care and Share Diamond" in every Christ follower's heart. Reading *God's Amazing Normal* takes you on a diamond-mining adventure in which God uses Larry's life transforming stories and scriptural calls to action to uncover and ignite the Prayer Care and Share diamond in your life.

Whatever type of shepherd or sheep you are and whatever level on the Prayer Care and Share Lifestyle barometer you are living at, Larry's book will propel you into the next level of radiating and reproducing the light and life of Christ for the expansion of His kingdom and the glory of our Lord Jesus Christ.

Larry, I thank you for and accept your challenge, dear Brother, to train trainers that will live and reproduce the prayer care and share lifestyle for the glory of our King Jesus.

Colin C. Millar

Chief Prayer Officer (CPO) for GMO, Global Media Outreach a partner with Campus Crusade for Christ

# # # # #

Larry DeWitt has given us a must-read, refreshingly written book that gives us practical ways to bring back into focus what the church and every Christian is to be about. Having been mentored by Pastor DeWitt at Calvary Community Church, I saw the way he lived out in person and in leadership what it means to lift up Christ and help as many people as possible be ready for His return. The result was a rapidly growing church that touched thousands of lives . . . my own included. I believe his book will do the same.

Linus Morris

Founder, Christian Associates International and

On Expedition

GOD'S AMAZING NORMAL

Introduction

—◊—

Take a walk back through your most exhilarating moments in life. Some of those moments are probably about physical birth and the awe you felt when you first looked at a newborn. Beccy and I remember the day our children were born like it

> *The most exciting thing on earth is birth!*

happened yesterday; their births changed everything . . . forever. Recently I watched my granddaughter playing with her first doll. She was already practicing being a mom! *The most exciting thing on earth is birth!*

Likewise, remember your spiritual birth, when you first became alive in Christ. The most exciting experiences spiritually are moments of birth and new life in Christ. Every living thing God created has the capacity to reproduce; it's normal and joyful. God has given us the capacity to reproduce spiritually, so why don't we? So, why do a majority of

Christ followers say they have never helped someone else come alive in Christ?

When I left the mother church of my denomination and moved to California, I embraced the challenge of helping believers reproduce spiritually. During my 27 years of pastoring Calvary Community, God allowed the church to grow from six families to thousands, many of them new followers of Christ. Later, in my role as national facilitator of pastoral ministries for the Mission America Coalition, I met with pastors and leaders in many cities across America. The challenge? To help those church leaders prepare believers to love others to life in Christ.

This book is a proposal for a new and effective DNA in churches. It's time to get the monkey off the pastors' backs and allow them to be shepherds. Shepherds don't make sheep; they nurture sheep so that they become mature and reproduce. Healthy sheep have lambs. Sheep happen!

Imagine a fresh DNA in followers of Jesus where reproducing our life in Christ is normal. Imagine churches and believers who:

- Stay focused on Christ
- Are driven by Christ's mission
- Reproduce . . . it's normal
- Let Christ's light shine
- Pray . . . care . . . share

- Live a pray-care-share lifestyle

- Get practical

- Live ready—Christ is coming

Until He comes, I dream about the joy of seeing my grandchildren grow up and have the joy of birthing children. I also dream about seeing God's children mature and have the joy of birthing others into a new life in Christ! Not only is this Christ's command and one of the most exhilarating experiences in life, but it is also God's amazing and fulfilling normal!

Larry DeWitt

Chapter 1

STAY FOCUSED ON CHRIST

—⁓—

I remember the film *City Slickers*. It was about a midlife-plagued man and his friends who were searching for renewal and purpose on a cattle-driving vacation under the leadership of wise trail boss, "Curly." Every night at campfire time, Curly would say: "Do you know what the secret of life is? Just . . . one . . . thing. You stick to that and everything else means nothing."

Mitch: "That's great but, what's the one thing?"

Curly: "That's what you've got to figure out."

You may be asking yourself, What are the important things for me to do this week? without asking, *What's the important thing for me to do on earth?*

Life Is Knowing and Staying Focused on the Main Thing

When I was finishing seminary, I talked with Warren Thompson, senior pastor at the church where I was youth and music director. I asked him my profound question: "What are the important things you'd like to say to a young man

Make much of Jesus Christ!

about to go out and begin his ministry?" I was waiting for his list!

This very gifted Bible teacher didn't hesitate but said, "Just remember one thing . . . make much of Jesus Christ." Little did I realize then that the most important thing I learned while I was in seminary was not what I learned in seminary. It was what I learned from this pastor. That statement became a motto for my life: ***Make much of Jesus Christ!***

In our lives and in our churches there can be so much clutter. As a leader, I realized that I needed to continually refocus on the main thing. That's the deal of leadership: What's the main thing?

Jesus Christ's life—His crucifixion, burial, and resurrection—is not only an important message of history, it is the *essential* message of history. I believe the main thing in life is that we encounter and follow Christ. We need to be overwhelmed by His grace, receive His forgiveness, recognize His love, and see Him as the source of life and the ultimate hope for the future. The Apostle Paul put it this way:

I have been crucified with Christ and I no longer live, but Christ lives in me. The life I live in the body, I live by faith in the Son of God, who loved me and gave himself for me. I do not set aside the grace of God, for if righteousness could be gained through the law, Christ died for nothing! (Galatians 2:20-21)

I hear people talk about being part of . . .

- a Bible-centered church, where the focus is God's written Word

- a prayer-centered church, where the focus is being a "house of prayer"

- a Spirit-centered church, where God manifests Himself through His Holy Spirit

- a worship-centered church, where we're all about worshiping our Holy God

- a people-centered church, where it's all about meeting people's needs

- a community-centered church, where we're primarily here for the community

All that I've mentioned in this list are important—very important. But I don't believe any of them is the center. I believe in a Christ-centered life and church—where Jesus Christ is the center of everything!

I have a son named Kirk. As a pastor, Kirk loves people and has a profound ministry in helping believers serve and show the love of Christ to other people. I clearly remember speaking at a church in the Bay Area at the same time my son was speaking at Calvary Community, the church I founded. I had difficulty focusing on my teaching assignment because my heart was more focused on my son's teaching and his ministry that day. In my heart I knew I would rather see my son be blessed and be a blessing than to receive a blessing myself. If you are a parent, it should be no surprise to you that God the Father is pleased to have the focus on His Son. He has declared Jesus Christ to be the center and focus of the Church.

Paul understood and was clearly committed to the one thing, the one Person, Jesus Christ. Listen to his resolve:

And so it was with me, brothers and sisters. When I came to you, I did not come with eloquence or human wisdom as I proclaimed to you the testimony about God. For I resolved to know nothing while I was with you except Jesus Christ and him crucified. I came to you in weakness with great fear and trembling. My message and my preaching were not with wise and persuasive words, but with a demonstration of the Spirit's power, so that your faith might not rest on human wisdom, but on God's power. (1 Corinthians 2:1-5)

As a pastor I often came to Christ in weakness, fear, and with much trembling. When teaching, I often found myself wondering, *Is what I'm about to say persuasive enough? Strong and compelling? How will people respond?* The ongoing challenge during this time was to get the focus off of myself and my apprehension and to keep it clearly on Christ. Then I was to trust the Holy Spirit to penetrate people's hearts and lives with the life of our incredible Christ.

A Christian church is a gathering of people in Christ's name. How is it possible to experience an entire set of praise music that is focused on God the Father but never mentions Jesus Christ? Christ is more than the complimentary close at the end of a prayer—"in the name of Jesus we pray." He's more than a reference in the footnotes—He is *the message.*

I have adopted, as my own, Paul's resolve "to know nothing while I was with you except Jesus Christ and him crucified" (1 Corinthians 2:2). Paul obviously did not mean that he knew nothing else; he did mean that this was the essential message. Like Paul, I've resolved in my life to never stop refocusing on the wonder of Christ's rescue of my life. I believe God the Father has decreed, with several beautiful illustrations in the New Testament, that Jesus Christ is to be the center of our focus in the Church.

Scriptures that have given me such strong conviction about this are:

1. **Christ Is the Head of the Church**

"God placed all things under his feet and appointed him to be head over everything for the church." (Ephesians 1:22)

As a pastor I would frequently ask, "What would Jesus Christ, the head of the church, want us to do about this?" When we talk about vision and mission, we don't need to start from scratch. We start with what His vision and heart for this world is. The church should be all about Jesus and His vision. The same should be true for our personal lives. When we talk about our personal and family decisions, do we ask each other, "What would Jesus like us to do?"

2. **Christ Is the Cornerstone**

"Christ Jesus himself [is] the chief cornerstone. In him the whole building is joined together and rises to become a holy temple to the Lord." (Ephesians 2:20-21)

The foundation of life individually and of life together as the church is Jesus Christ. He's the reference point— where it starts. If the foundation isn't right, the rest of it will be wrong.

When I was a young pastor in Orangevale, California, I remember the day the builders laid out the foundation for our new church building. I watched them identify the first corner of the building; but somehow I felt it was not right. So,

I went out after lunch and talked to the builder, who assured me that it was right. But I couldn't let go of it. We continued to talk until, finally, he realized it was ten feet too close to the property line and if they had proceeded the whole building would have been wrong and in violation of code.

I have thought about that experience and the importance of having a true cornerstone a hundred times since then. Take a look at your life and ask, "Is it clear that Jesus is the foundation and the reference point for everything?" If Christ is not the cornerstone of life, the rest of it will be wrong. What does it mean for Christ to be the cornerstone of your relationships, your finances, your work, for every area of your life?

3. **The Church Is Christ's Bride**

In Ephesians 5, there is a passage entitled "Wives and Husbands." It is about the roles of wife and husband; but near the end of the passage Paul says: "This is a profound mystery—but I am talking about Christ and the church" (v. 32). The greatest reflection of our relationship to Christ should be the way a husband and wife relate to each other. Jesus Christ loves the Church and gave Himself up for her. When I find myself thinking that I am making a great sacrifice for Beccy, my wife, I remember that Christ literally gave up His life for me.

Christian marriage should be the best demonstration on earth of Christ's love for us and our loyalty to Him. I believe the best teaching I ever gave at Calvary was not my words but letting the people see my love and devotion for

> *Give Christ the supremacy in everything.*

Beccy. Do people see the similarity in my love and loyalty to Christ? This timeless hymn beautifully describes Christ's devotion for His Bride, the church:

The church's one foundation is Jesus Christ her Lord;
She is his new creation by water and the Word.
From heaven he came and sought her to be his holy bride;
With his own blood he bought her, and for her life he died.
Text: Samuel J. Stone, 1839-1900
Music: Samuel Sebastian Wesley, 1810-1876

4. **Christ Is Supreme in Everything About the Church**

In him all things were created . . . all things have been created through him and for him.

"He is the head of the body, the church . . . so that in everything he might have the supremacy. God was pleased to have all his fullness dwell in him. (Colossians 1:16,18-19)

Colossians 1 leaves no question: God the Father has specifically said that we are to *give Christ the supremacy in everything*—in our praise, in our teaching, in our relationships. He IS our VIP and the Church's VIP . . . and God likes it that way. To me this is the most comprehensive expression in Scripture regarding Christ's place in the church.

8

For as long as I was pastor of a church, I would pray every Sunday, *"Lord Jesus, if somebody walks in here today, and never comes back again, may they know that Jesus Christ is the VIP around this place."* It's important to ask ourselves this question: If someone walked out of the service we attended last Sunday and asked, "What's the main thing here this morning?" would the answer clearly be, "Jesus Christ—it's really all about Him!"? And, if others were to look at your life today, would they see that Jesus Christ is your VIP?

THINK ABOUT IT . . .

1. In what areas of your life are you challenged to let Christ have the last word?

2. As others look at your life, what indicates that Jesus Christ is your VIP?

Chapter 2

BE DRIVEN BY CHRIST'S MISSION

—ɯ—

D o we remember where we came from? Where we were when God picked us up, rescued us, and said I'm going to use you? I'd encourage each of us to go back frequently and recall that life-changing time. Why? It helps us to refocus on Christ and His grace with gratitude.

For me, part of staying focused on Christ is going back to my beginnings and remembering what Jesus Christ did for

> *Remembering when Christ rescued us will help us have the heart of Christ for other people.*

me as a teen when I was so lost. I had no sense of what life was about. I had literally no dreams and vision about my future. Christ sought me out, rescued me, and instantly gave me a sense of identity with His life purpose:

To help others discover what I found in Christ . . .

Forgiveness. Hope. Meaning. Future. Purpose.

To help me recall my own beginnings, I occasionally look at the story of King David. As an older man of God he was well settled in his palace, thinking about building a grandiose temple for God. The word of the Lord came to Nathan the prophet, and he asked David, "Do you remember where you came from? When you were a scrawny little kid, shepherding sheep on the hillsides near Bethlehem? Your dad didn't think you were even worthy of notice in comparison with your other brothers. When the prophet came looking for a king, you weren't on the radar screen. But I took you from the pasture and from following the flock to be ruler over my people Israel. I've been with you wherever you've gone" (1 Chronicles 17, author's paraphrase).

Remembering when Christ rescued us will help us have the heart of Christ for other people who need to be rescued. It's a reminder that Christ alone transformed us, and He transforms others. Our sense of grace and gratitude drives us with passion to want to see others know and experience His grace and forgiveness. Martin Luther daily went back to his beginnings with Christ, reportedly saying, "I feel as if Jesus had died only yesterday."[1]

How often do we reflect on and share with others how God rescued us?

Lord, may we never get over our gratitude for Your love, forgiveness, and salvation.

12

We All Get Lost

I get lost quite frequently. In a large city in Italy, Beccy and I needed to board a train. We went to what we thought was the right track to our destination. We saw the train arriving from that destination and assumed it was going to pick up passengers, leave, and return there. After the

> *Lord, may we never get over our gratitude for Your love, forgiveness, and salvation.*

passengers disembarked we were the first ones to board the train. Actually, we were the *only* ones.

Shortly thereafter, we heard a click and the train was locked. We were helplessly and hopelessly stuck inside with no way to get out. We realized this train wasn't going anywhere. We were lost. We pounded on the windows. Finally we found an open window and yelled to a conductor. He came over and chewed us out in Italian, hand motions and all. He finally let us out and pointed us in the right direction. What a relief! We just didn't want to spend our time in Italy stuck in a deserted train.

When someone is lost they don't need to be condemned or rebuked for their mistake. **Lost people simply need help.** We don't get lost because we're bad. We get lost because we don't know the way.

When was the last time you were lost? After several attempts, you knew you couldn't find your own way. You got your nerve up and asked for directions from somebody. You needed help. It doesn't mean you were evil; you simply had lost your way.

As Jesus made His final approach to Jerusalem just days before His Passion Week, He traveled through Jericho where

*L*ost people simply need help.

He invited Himself to dinner at the house of Zacchaeus, the chief tax collector. The event transformed Zacchaeus. Jesus stood up at the end of their dinner and stated to everyone His life's mission on earth: "The son of man came to *seek* and to *save* what was *lost*" (Luke 19:10, italics added).

- To "seek" means to take the initiative with people.
- To "save" literally means to rescue.
- "Lost" means you simply can't find your way.

Zacchaeus was lost. Jesus didn't rebuke him, He had dinner with him! And early the next day Jesus continued toward Jerusalem where He would lay down His life for all lost people.

So, if that's Christ's mission, I see laying down my life for lost people as my mission, too. I must take the initiative to help rescue people who have

*H*elp as many people as possible to be ready for Christ's return.

lost their way and don't know how to find it.

14

This was the motto we communicated at Calvary Community. It was clear and to the point:

To help as many people as possible

to be ready for Christ's return.

The mission was clear; the people caught it. It became personal. It helped them get past their focus on themselves and cooperate with Christ in helping others to know Christ and be ready for His return.

A Bit of History

In 1976, God led Beccy and me to Thousand Oaks in the Conejo Valley, California, where we were privileged to birth Calvary Community Church. God confirmed the mission of helping lost people find life in Christ. We began with six families, and the early days were very exciting with many people meeting Christ and growing in Him.

The first week we were there, we met with the director of the chamber of commerce and asked, "What's the most central, visible place where people come together in town?" He said it was Los Robles Country Club, where the Rotary and other community groups met. I asked, "What if our church met there?" He helped us to make that happen. We rented the banquet room and had a very exciting beginning. Would you believe, one of the first two people to meet Christ at that new church was the director of the chamber of commerce? He

15

had been unchurched and rather hostile toward the church. The other was an older gentleman whose wife and son had attended church all their lives. He wanted no part of it. Then, one Sunday morning, he surprised his family by saying, "I want to go with you to church this morning." After 30-plus years of resistance, he not only came to church, he came to Christ. That was the beginning of many people coming and discovering new life in Christ. The church grew significantly and within the first two years we had a few hundred people.

The day came when the restaurant manager approached me and said, "Reverend, we're not opposed to your having a church here, but we're trying to run a restaurant and there's simply not enough parking for the people. You need to leave within a month."

Now, let me fast-forward 30 years. Beccy and I had been out of town and returned in time for an evening dinner meeting. I had learned about an extreme home makeover that involved approximately 50 people from Calvary. I said to Beccy, "We're going to have to be late for that dinner meeting. I feel compelled to go look at this project." The makeover had been initiated by a group of teens who had been meeting for Bible study in the neighborhood. They had noticed a dilapidated house across the street, occupied by an older gentleman who was quite ill. They talked with their dads about doing something to help the man with his house.

16

I knew in my heart God wanted me to go see this project. I arrived at the house and saw that it was happening—landscaping, sidewalks, complete repainting of the exterior, windows repaired, new screens, etc. I was invited inside to meet the owner—a gentleman named John.

He asked me, "Do you remember me?"

I said, "No, I'm afraid I don't."

He said, "Well, I'm the guy who rented the Los Robles Country Club restaurant to you when you started that church 30 years ago. I never came to the church, but today your people came to me, and I met Jesus. I saw their love and kindness to me." He looked at me and said, "I'm in! I'm saved, and going to heaven! After 30 years, your church has changed my life."

The man who was leading this makeover project had never personally invited someone to follow Christ. He was ready to call a pastor but decided to just go ahead and talk when John asked.

John said, "He invited me to receive Christ, and I did."

John's excitement was not only that he had a new house but that Christ was at home in his heart. Even more exciting was to see the face of the man who had just shared with him. This man who came to help do a home makeover helped John to have a heart makeover.

John was able to come to Calvary just a few weeks after this event. I introduced him publicly. He shared with people that he had met Christ and thanked people for his new home.

Within a month, John went home to be with Christ.

The Journey Continues

Rewind to 30 years earlier. When John gave us a month's notice to leave the country club location, we scrambled to find a new home. We ended up in a new, vacant warehouse, which became our temporary home for many years. First a country club, then a warehouse—but where we met was not important. The mission was important. It was always about making room for the lost, who were searching to find the Way.

To make room for people who were coming to Christ, we looked for another, more permanent, location and actually bought some property along the freeway. I wanted to give people a vision of the future, so when we had a picnic on the property I arranged for a plane to fly overhead and sky-write the number 69661. On Sunday, I asked people if they could figure it out. What did it mean? I heard all kinds of ideas—it was the address, the square footage of a building, etc. No one guessed its meaning, so I told them: "That's the number, as best we knew, of unchurched *people* in our valley."

The point was to plant a vision in their heads and hearts of bringing *people* to Christ—not some percentage, not some growth number, but *people*. Unchurched *people*. It was a vision so large, so compassionate, and so Christ-centered that only God could do it.

Getting Personal

After years and many attempts we were unable to build on that property, so we bought a large industrial campus from the Eaton Corporation, which would become our new church home.

The elders said to me, "Pastor, you have a vision of reaching thousands of people in this valley. With due respect, that's nice, but we're not sure the people see that vision. Find a way to make it personal—so that every single person can own a part of that vision."

The elders taught me a lot that day. It was not just a matter of the pastor having a God-given vision; the *people* must also own and participate in it.

Someone on the staff said, "Everyone needs to feel that the mission is about reaching people, not about a big building." He suggested, "Why don't we just write on the wall of this warehouse the names of people we know who need to know Christ?"

And we did just that. In a very real sense the wall became our "wailing wall"—a place we focused for prayer. Our holy graffiti.

For the next month, I asked the congregation to go to the wall during praise time and write names of people who seemed lost, people who needed to find Christ. In a matter of a month there were almost 27,000 names (first names only) on that wall. *People*—not buildings and dollars—became the focus for our new home. I remember looking at that wall and saying to the congregation, "That's not just a wall of 27,000 names. Every single name on that wall means something to someone here. Each name is a father, a mother, a brother, a child, a neighbor, a business associate, a friend at the club, a schoolmate." The people's focus had changed from wanting a new building to wanting a place where there would be room for people we truly cared about to come together as a family in Christ and follow Him.

I would frequently go to that wall in a creative way. I would walk to the wall during a celebration service and say, "Let's pray for the people whose names are on this wall. Let's go to the wall for them." Sometimes I'd ask, "Who has a mother's name written on this wall?" I'd ask people to raise their hands. It became so personal when everyone took just one minute to pray for moms to know Christ. Everybody in the room was touched. Sometimes we prayed for neighbors or business associates, and we always gave the opportunity for people to add more names to the wall. I frequently clarified why we went to the wall; we went so that the people we had committed to praying for personally would also be prayed for by the whole family of God. We would join each other in praying that they too would meet Christ.

One Sunday I mentioned the wall and praying for neighbors and friends whose names were on the wall. One family had brought their neighbors to church for the first time. When I mentioned the wall, the neighbors leaned over and whispered to them, "Are our names on that wall?"

That church family froze with fear that they'd offended and embarrassed their neighbors, but they reluctantly admitted, "Yes."

After the service, the neighbors said to the church family who had brought them, "Could we see our names on the wall?"

They walked together over to the wall, and the church family pointed to the neighbors' names on the wall, waiting apprehensively.

Their guests said, "Do you mean you care enough about us that you put our names up there and you've been praying for us to find Christ?"

"Yes."

These two families stood there together, and the church family prayed with their neighbors to meet Christ, literally standing next to their names on a prayer wall.

I'm tearful just sharing that story with you. But, as amazing and moving as it is, the best of it was a Sunday some weeks later, when I was able to introduce both couples to the congregation and let them tell their story. How do you think that impacted the Body that morning? It went right to the jugular. Nothing is more

> *Let's spend time remembering on a regular basis the joy and excitement when we first reached out to take Christ's hand.*

powerful than a personally shared story of meeting Christ. By the way, later that family baptized their neighbors. Why didn't I do it? The answer is that *they* were the spiritual "parents" who had helped their neighbors come to Christ and would help them grow in Christ.

We began encouraging people to be baptized by whoever helped them come to Christ. We took time in celebrations to hear not only the confessions of faith of people who were being baptized, but also the story of the person who became light and showed them the way to Christ. This was also saying to the church family that we can all be a part of helping others around us come to Christ and experience the great joy of spiritual birth. It's amazing in a church family to have everybody thinking about their neighbors or their friends or loved ones who need to know Christ and encouraging each other to believe that it can really happen.

Almost every week I interviewed someone who told their story of how Christ touched them or used them in someone else's life. This is hard to say, but I came to believe that people learned more from hearing stories of Christ at work than they did from my sermons!

When Christ said "I, when I am lifted up from the earth, will draw all men to myself" (John 12:32), we know He was talking about His crucifixion. It's literally true that when Jesus Christ is lifted up in the church—who He is and what He's done and His rightful place in our lives—people will be drawn to Him.

In summary . . . It's so very easy in life's hustle and bustle to forget where we've come. ***Let's spend time remembering on a regular basis the joy and excitement when we first reached out to take Christ's hand***—that moment when He pulled us from our sins and failures and gave us hope and life.

THINK ABOUT IT . . .

1. How often do you go back to your beginning and express gratitude to Christ for rescuing you? What prompts you to do that?

2. How are you joining Christ in His mission of seeking and rescuing lost people? How have you done that in the past week? How can you do it in the future?

Chapter 3

REPRODUCE . . . IT'S NORMAL

—ᴍ—

A profound principle in the creation story in Genesis is that to every living thing God created, He gave a capacity to reproduce. "Be fruitful and increase in number" (1:22,28). And what's true for the animal kingdom is true for man. It's part of God's blessing . . . Be fruitful and multiply.

Shepherd and Sheep

Throughout Scripture, God's leaders are often referred to as shepherds. And for many this is exactly what they were— Abel, Abraham, Joseph, Moses, David, and others were all shepherds. Christ also calls Himself the Great Shepherd. He gives His life up for His sheep; He protects them; He leads them in and out to find healthy pastures. And, like any good shepherd, He expects His sheep to produce more sheep.

Pastors are also shepherds. I was in Ciudad Juarez, Mexico, with the president of Campus Crusade, talking to pastors about shepherds and sheep. I said, "Supposing you were a shepherd." The translator stopped me and said, "Shepherd and pastor—same word in Spanish." Aha. So, pastors *are* shepherds.

I continued, asking those pastors to consider, "Supposing

> S *heep produce sheep.*
> *Shepherds don't.*

you had a flock of 300 sheep and for two or three years there were no new lambs. What would you think? What would you do? What would need to change?"

Over the years I've thought a lot about my responsibilities as a shepherd to God's flock. I came to see that it was my responsibility to provide a healthy environment for nurturing and caring. I believed that, as they matured, they would reproduce. Lambs would happen. If not, something was wrong, and I needed to figure it out.

Here's a profound principle that I'm not sure all pastors understand:

Sheep produce sheep. Shepherds don't.

The principle of creation is that everything God gave life to He gave the capacity to reproduce. A shepherd of sheep would never say, *If only 10 percent reproduce, that's fine.* We certainly don't say that about human families, *It's fine if only 10 percent give birth to children.* Why should we say, in the church, that it's okay if only 10 percent of God's children reproduce their spiritual life? I believe it should be normal for all of God's children to be involved in seeing their spiritual life reproduced in others.

Not for Professionals

Unfortunately, we are more inclined to leave evangelism to the "pros," the pastor, the highly trained leaders. But there is a better way.

If someone walked up to me after a service and shared his interest in knowing Christ, I would pray, look around and find some established believer, introduce them to one another and say, "Tell him what you just told me. How about the two of you getting together and talking about what it means to know Christ."

A lady named Theresa called me and said, "Pastor, a neighbor I've prayed for and been a friend to for years is in the hospital, very sick with cancer. I think the time has come to talk to him about receiving Christ."

I was pretty sure she thought I or some professional should talk to him. But my response was, "You're his friend and neighbor. You're trusted. You're the one who has had a burden to see him come to Christ. For me to go now would be an intrusion at a very sensitive time."

Instead of going, I offered some suggestions of how she might initiate the conversation and how that encounter could happen, and I prayed for her, that she would help her neighbor and family find life and hope in Christ.

A week later, Theresa called me. She was so excited that God had allowed *her* the privilege of being there for her neighbor and bringing hope to him in the Lord. And later, she was there with his family through the grief and joy as he "graduated" to heaven.

The most exciting thing on earth is birth. The most exciting thing in the church is rebirth!

Calvary Community Church was planted in the Conejo Valley in Southern California. What does the word "Conejo" mean? It means "rabbits." Rabbits are known for reproducing. I prayed that the church I pastored in the Conejo Valley would be known for reproducing.

Share the Joy

I remember the day when I was shaken by 1 Corinthians 1:15, where Paul said, "I am thankful that I did not baptize any of you except Crispus and Gaius, so no one can say that you were baptized in my name." Then he added, "I don't remember if I baptized anyone else" (v. 16). At Calvary, I recalled baptizing so many people that I could not begin to remember their names. I felt terrible. I was hoarding all the joy. I realized that their identity needed to be with Christ, *and with the people who helped them come to Christ.* Not with me.

So, I said to the congregation, "I want to stop baptizing people at Calvary." When I said that, I saw the shock go through the congregation. Then I said, "I think people should be baptized by whoever helped them come to Christ." Later, as I watched these baptisms, I asked the question: Who has the greater joy? The person being baptized or the spiritual parent who's baptizing them? As the congregation witnessed this approach to baptism, it stirred up the desire in them and the confidence to believe that they could help others find life in Christ as well.

Parents Nurture

There is a parenting instinct to nurture that comes with the birthing process. Just as it's natural for mothers to care for their newborns, I believe it's natural for spiritual parents to have a desire to nurture and care for their newborn in Christ. Yes, pastors need to give some resources, training, and coaching to these spiritual parents, but the parents are the ones to encourage spiritual growth and experience the joy that comes with spiritual parenting. ***Children learn best by walking with their parents; and*** likewise, ***spiritual children learn best by walking with their spiritual parents.***

An expectant mother may be scared to death about the responsibility of knowing how to care for a baby. Then the baby comes. And with it comes the physical capacity and instinct to care for and nurture that child as well. Likewise, if followers of Christ enter into labor and birth new life in Christ, they will have a God-given instinct and capacity to nurture them.

I recently talked to a global Christian leader who shared the story of a church movement that's now 15 years old and already has 20 new generations of churches. That means within seven or eight months a church generated a new church, so they have experienced exponential growth. A handful of people has become thousands, who will reproduce themselves in less than a year. This is a norm in many countries around the world—Beccy and I discovered this at a global Call2All event in Hong Kong 2009. Leaders were gathered from 110 nations. We realized that for many of them, seeing followers of Christ reproduce themselves in others—often within months or years—was just normal. I came home thinking that we in the American church are the ones who are more abnormal.

> *Children learn best by walking with their parents; and spiritual children learn best by walking with their spiritual parents.*

New DNA

There will be fresh, new DNA in our spiritual lives when we understand our roles. The role of a pastor-shepherd is to provide the right pasture—an environment of protection and nourishment. The role of the people is to then spiritually reproduce. In your life, to have new DNA means there has been a change in you—you see your role as being a reproductive follower of Christ.

When pastoring at Calvary Community, I was blessed to see many people bringing their family members and their friends to Christ. I felt great release as a pastor from a burden that God never expected me to carry. I found great joy in watching spiritual children reproduce themselves in others.

God has given you the amazing capacity to reproduce life—spiritual life.

Christ gave the commandment: "Therefore go and make disciples" (Matthew 28:16). I believe every person who is a follower of Christ is to be engaged in a process of helping others come to Christ and become His disciples. The role of pastor-shepherds is to help people know *how*. The role of followers of Christ is to anticipate the joy of reproducing.

Expect that as you grow in your faith in Christ you will have the great joy of helping others you love find life in Christ. **God has given you the amazing capacity to reproduce life—** physical life, but also the **spiritual life** He has given you.

Reproduce . . . it's normal!

THINK ABOUT IT . . .

1. What will need to change for you to see yourself as a reproducing Christian?

2. Who in your life right now can you walk with in their spiritual journey?

Chapter 4

LET CHRIST'S LIGHT SHINE

—ɯ—

W hat are the first recorded words of God in the Bible? "Let there be light."

In the beginning God created the heavens and the earth. Now the earth was formless and empty, darkness was over the surface of the deep, and the Spirit of God was hovering over the waters. And God said, *"Let there be light,"* and there was light. God saw that the light was good, and he separated the light from the darkness. (Genesis 1:1-4, italics added)

In creation, God gave light to the world. In verse 2, three words describe what the earth was like before light:

- Formless—a wasteland with no shape or order or purpose.
- Empty—there was no life. It was uninhabitable.
- Dark—darkness ruled over the surface of the deep.

At creation:

- Light brought order.

- Light made life possible.
- Light dispelled the darkness.

There's a very interesting parallel in the beginning of the book of Genesis and the beginning of the Gospel of John.

In the beginning was the Word, and the Word was with God, and the Word was God. He was with God in the beginning. Through him all things were made; without him nothing was made that has been made. In him was life, and that life was the light of men. The light shines in the darkness, but the darkness has not understood it. The true light that gives light to every man was coming into the world. (John 1:1-5,9)

- *In Genesis*, "In the beginning God" is talking about physical creation.
  - *In John*, "In the beginning was the Word [Jesus Christ]" is talking about spiritual re-creation.
- *In Genesis*, God created physical light, "Let there be light."
  - *In John*, God sent His Son to be the Light of the world.
- *In Genesis*, life was empty, purposeless, and dark before light was created.
  - *In John*, Life was without meaning and dark-ness ruled . . . until people discover Christ as the Light of the world.

In John 8, Jesus showed up at the Feast of the Tabernacles in Jerusalem and made an incredible claim. The opening illumination ceremony involved four torches that were lit and placed in the corners of the temple area for seven days of celebration.

"I am the light of the world!"

People danced all night before the Lord, celebrating God's light that led them from slavery in Egypt to the Promised Land. In some ways I think it was like the opening ceremony for the Olympics and the eternal torch.

At this festival, Jesus had the audacity to yell to the crowd a shocking assertion: *"I am the light of the world!"* What he was really saying was:

- I am not a light but the light;
- I'm greater than the light in the temple area;
- I'm greater than the lights in Jerusalem;
- I'm greater than the light that you are celebrating—the light that led the children of Israel from the desert to the Promised Land;
- I am light to the whole world—not just to the people of Jerusalem; not just to Jewish people; but to everyone who would and could believe.

Can you imagine how this claim shocked the people at the festival? At the end of seven days the lights in the corners of the temple went out and people went home; but the light of Christ continued to shine.

With that claim He made an incredible promise that I love to personalize:

"Whoever follows me will never walk in darkness but will have the light of life."

People who find and follow Christ may have dark days; but they won't be in the dark about the meaning of life. They literally have found the Light of life for now and eternity. Jesus Christ, the

> **"Whoever follows me will never walk in darkness but will have the light of life."**

Light, brings purpose: life has new meaning; darkness no longer rules over our lives. He changes everything.

This was true in my own life. When I first found Christ, I found reason for being and serving. I found a future, and life took on meaning. I remember as a teen coming to my senior year at Wheaton Academy, so lost, with no sense of purpose and really no hope about the future. In a matter of months I met Christ. I met Beccy who later became my wife. Everything changed. The light turned on; I was alive. I had a sense of purpose and mission. The message of 2 Corinthians 5:17 happened in me: "Therefore, if anyone is in Christ, he is a new creation; the old has gone, the new has come!" I was no longer in the dark about having hope in life. I began praying for other people to experience light and life in Christ. I had new drive and passion in my life that was nonexistent before I met Christ, and it has never left me. Jesus Christ truly became the light of my life.

In the next chapter, John 9, it is recorded that Jesus healed a blind man. When he was questioned by the authorities, he didn't know a lot about Jesus, but he did say, "One thing I do know. I was blind but now I see" (v. 25). The light Christ gave him changed *everything* about his life.

Later, Jesus qualified his statement by saying, **"While I am in the world, I am the light of the world"** (vv. 4-5). The implication is clear: He would not always be here to be that light, but the light won't go away. How is that possible?

How Did Jesus Leave, but His Light Remain?

Part of the answer can be found in the Sermon on the Mount, where Jesus made another astounding statement: **"*You* are the light of the world**" (Matthew 5:18). He said this not just to His disciples but to a large crowd of people. He went on to say your light would be: **Like a city.** "A town built on a hill cannot be hidden" (Matthew 5:14). Everyone listening to Him

> **"*You* are the light of the world."**

knew He was referring to the city of Safat. It was the compass for the fishermen and people of Capernaum. It was a city on a hill for travelers and seamen to get their bearings—north-northwest—when they were out on the Sea of Galilee fishing at night. The city was consistently there; they could count on it. It helped them find their way back to shore.

I believe that Jesus was talking about a wonderful partnership between Him and us. I believe He was saying, *Together My light, shining through each of you, will give an aura, a warmth, a hope to cities and to lives of people in the world where you live. Like Safat, true light will be consistent; it will always be there for them; it will give them their bearings. Through you, My light will be their compass.*

When you fly into a city at night, you see an aura of light over it. But as you get closer to landing, you realize that aura is really thousands, maybe millions, of lights that together give a glow and illuminate the city. Whenever I fly at night and approach a city, I see that glow and pray about the lights that make up that aura; and I think about Christ's desire that in every city, every community, His lights—the followers of Christ—will be consistent, bringing radiance and hope to their community.

Continuing with the Sermon on the Mount, Christ provided an even more personal illustration, saying we are **like a lamp**. He said, "Neither do people light a lamp and put it under a bowl. Instead they put it on its stand, and it gives light to everyone in the house" (Matthew 5:15).

Homes in the Middle East were quite dark, often having only one room, one window and one source of light. It wasn't easy to start a fire, so they kept the lamp going day and night. When they weren't using the lamp during the day, they put it under a bowl or in a protected place just to keep it burning. When darkness came, they took out their lamp, set it on a pedestal in the middle of the room, and it gave light to everything and everyone in the house. Imagine your family gathering in one small room of your house, with one candle lit in the middle of it. Think about the radiance, the warmth, the light it would give to the entire family. In the Middle East, every dinner was by candlelight.

So, what was Jesus really saying about us being His light? He was saying that we're here to bring light when it's dark to the people around us; to bring a sense of warmth, radiance, and even

So, let Christ's light shine!

guidance. Jesus calls for every follower to be part of His light on earth, and through them, His radiance will shine on every-body around them.

So, let Christ's light shine! Let it shine in the darkness.

A Simple Strategy

Next He gave them a very simple strategy: **"In the same way, let your light shine before men, that they may**

see your good deeds and praise your Father in heaven" (Matthew 5:16). Jesus was really saying, Here's how it will work: You let your light shine through the good deeds you do for people—all kinds of people, anyone around you—by serving and loving. The result may well be they will "praise your Father in heaven." When people see your love and think about your kindness and goodness to them, hopefully their focus will be on "Why are you being so kind or gracious to me?" And they'll end up thinking about the God who gave you that kind of love and concern for them.

A younger neighbor of ours was going through a divorce. Much of the time his two children were at the house. I was one of the few people who would actually strike up a conversation with him. I think my "good deeds" to him was merely asking him how he was doing, how the kids were doing, how tough it was being alone with two kids; and merely listening and letting him know that I cared. We talked about those things, and about what was going on with his career. One day he asked me why I was so nice to him.

I answered, "I know it must be tough for you, and I care about you." I think I even threw in a God sentence, "God loves you, and so do I." Pretty soon his kids were calling us Uncle Larry and Aunt Beccy. And, in time, he began asking questions about Christ and about life.

"You are the light of the world"—what an astounding statement. And to understand how to be that light, we have to understand how Jesus was that light. Do we love people as He loves them? Do we show them compassion, grace, mercy, concern? How much radiance of Christ are we reflecting to others around us?

One day an older neighbor, who had recently moved in, walked by our home. She was visibly upset and I asked if she was okay. She replied, "Oh, I'm having a tough time living here. The house I raised my kids in and lived in for 30-plus years has not sold. It's been on the market for months. I don't know what to do."

I showed interest and felt prompted by the Holy Spirit to ask, "Could we pray with you about it?"

She said, "Sure." So Beccy and I prayed with her. "God, give courage to our neighbor; and we pray that you'll help with the need to sell her previous home, and help her to feel good about living here."

> *Be a friend, and ask, How can I help?*

A couple days later she again walked by and said, "You won't believe what happened. The day after we prayed, my house sold! I've got friends who want to come and pray with you!"

41

I tell this story not to say anything about me, but to say something about the power of prayer and about having the courage to just reach out, **be a friend, and ask, How can I help?**

You Are a Lighthouse

What is the purpose of lighthouses? Is it just to add scenic beauty to the shorelines? Lighthouses were intentionally built to provide safety and harbor and help people get their bearings in the fog. Much of that task has been replaced today by electronic harbor markers and GPS, but the principle is the same.

I was boating in the Pacific, heading toward Newport Beach harbor for the first time. A heavy fog rolled in and we couldn't see farther that 50 feet. Slowly we moved toward what we thought was the channel into the harbor when I saw a rocky breakwater and the red harbor light to our left! If you know boating rules, you know about "red-right—return." The red harbor light must be on your right to enter the harbor. We were in serious trouble but were able to make the correction and get into the harbor safely. The first thing on my mind was . . . go to West Marine and buy some new GPS navigation equipment!

The next Sunday I told this story of being lost and in jeopardy at sea, and of vowing never to go to sea again without a well-functioning GPS. After the church service a man came up to me and said to me, "I own and distribute the GPS product you bought. When you told your story I realized that I have helped many people in trouble at sea; but I am lost, and my life and all I have is in danger of being destroyed."

People don't need a lighthouse or harbor markers during the day or when the weather is fine. But guess what? When it's dark and they need their bearings, it's important the harbor lights are there for them.

> *The light shines brightest when the world is darkest.*

So also, it's imperative for people around us to know that if life gets dark and they're looking for someone or something to give them some bearings, we can be that light to them. ***The light shines brightest when the world is darkest.***

So, let His light shine. Shinc it!

THINK ABOUT IT . . .

1. Who needs to see Christ's light in you?
   - Family?
   - Friends and neighbors?
   - People at work or school?
2. How can you be Christ's light?

Chapter 5

PRAY . . . CARE . . . SHARE

—ɯ—

I was on a conference call with Steve Douglass, president of Campus Crusade for Christ International. He said to the group, "It's as simple as this: imagine every believer—praying, caring, and sharing."

The simple strategy of **pray-care-share** has been the clear framework for Mission America Coalition, with whom I've had the privilege of serving as National Facilitator for Pastors. Mission America has encouraged this basic model for believers in cities all over the nation. I've been blessed to serve in many cities on behalf of Mission America, encouraging pastors to come together around a singular vision of Loving Communities to Christ through praying, caring, and sharing. Can you imagine what would happen if every follower of Christ were praying for people by name, caring by showing love and serving people, and available to share Christ in whatever way seemed appropriate?

45

Beccy and I had the privilege of meeting with the leaders of a dozen national women's ministries that had a combined participation of 3.2 million women. We shared together the concept of praying, caring, and sharing. Then I asked each of these ladies, Which of those efforts does your ministry emphasize most? All of them could easily identify a ministry—teaching women the Bible, or about prayer, or about benevolence and compassion, or sharing the gospel.

I asked, "Which of you is doing all three—praying, caring, *and* sharing? Could the ministry you lead focus on praying, caring, and sharing without losing your unique emphasis? If so, what would happen to women's ministries in America?"

One of them clearly stated, "It would radically change our impact on women in America."

Ask yourself the same question: If you could balance praying for people who need to meet Christ . . . caring and loving people in Christ's name . . . and appropriately sharing a challenge to put their faith in Christ—what would happen?

A camera is set on a tripod to keep it in focus. All three legs of the tripod are essential and must be balanced. Otherwise, tripods just don't work. I believe the same is true of our outreach. All three "legs" of pray-care-share need to be happening for our lives to be effective and balanced in helping people come to Christ.

I believe **these concepts of pray, care, and share are applicable for any culture, any age, for traditional churches or fresh young models of church life.** In one city, as I shared these concepts, among those listening were young pastors who were developing new models of church life. Their response to this idea of everyone praying,

> *These concepts of pray, care, and share are applicable for any culture, any age, for traditional churches or fresh young models of church life.*

caring, and sharing was: "This seems so right-on to us. Our generation sees evangelism as relational and based on authentic caring for and loving people. It really makes a lot of sense to us."

There are three simple actions that *every* believer can take to let Jesus shine . . .

1. **Pray for people by name**. We are exhorted in Paul's letter to Timothy, "I urge, then, first of all, that requests, prayers, intercession and thanksgiving be made for everyone" (1 Timothy 2:1). Write down names of family members, neighbors, friends, those at work and schoolmates whom the Holy Spirit puts on your heart. Now, we're not called to judge anyone—only God knows people's hearts—but we are called to pray for people and to care about people. "Devote yourselves to prayer . . . that God may open a door . . . that we may proclaim . . . Christ" (Colossians 4:2-3).

Get specific in your prayers, and God will be specific in His answers. There's a world of difference in saying, "God help people in my town come to Christ" and identifying specific people God puts on your heart and praying for them personally, individually—by name. Who's on your mind right now? Do you have a brother or sister or mother or father who

> ***Get specific in your prayers, and God will be specific in His answers.***

doesn't have a relationship with Christ? Do you have neighbors or friends or work associates you're concerned about? What if you start praying regularly for them, specifically, by name?

2. **Care for people**. Christ said, "Love your neighbor as yourself" (Mark 12:31). Show care and interest in others; seek to serve them. Watch for needs, for opportunities. Be intentional about seeking to help people and serve. When you pray for people by name, pray, *Lord, help me to find a way to value them, to serve, and to show Your love to them. Help me to take the time to do it.* Sometimes the best way to care is just to listen and learn, and value another person. I'm amazed at how open relationships are with some of my neighbors simply because I have taken time to talk about what's happening in their lives and discover their interests. Frankly, sometimes it's as easy as taking time and being intentional with a mind focused on them rather than on myself.

3. **Share with people.** "Go into all the world and preach the good news to all creation" (Mark 16:15). As natural opportunities arise, share when God encourages you and in a way that you feel is appropriate. As you serve and show love to people, in time they will be wondering why. Pray that you'll recognize the time and opportunity. Sharing may be a word of encouragement, a sentence or two about what Christ means to you, or even telling your story of how you met Christ.

At Calvary Community, I taught this simple strategy of praying, caring, and sharing, and thousands of followers of Christ began to live a pray-care-share lifestyle. This strategy was intentional; it was really about joining Christ in His mission to seek and to save lost people.

Have a list of people you are praying for; seek to serve those people in some way; and share your faith when and as appropriate. It's not asking "Do I know enough?" "Do I have the gift of evangelism?" or "How will I know what to say?" It simply comes down to something everyone of us can do.

Here is a very simple prayer to pray for yourself—every day:

Lord, help me to . . .

- be consistent in my walk,

*- be persistent in my **prayers** for people,*

*- see opportunities to **care** for people,*

*- know the right way and time to **share** Christ with them.*

Now, offer a prayer for each person on your prayer list by name.

Lord, I pray that _____ will come to know Christ; that they will experience Your forgiveness and freedom, and will live in Your love and hope.

As praying, caring, and sharing become a part of our spiritual DNA, just imagine what will happen. We will be changed. The focus no longer will be on us, but on joining Christ in His mission and on others. We will see God change things—first of all us, and then other people we love. When we cooperate with Christ and join Him in His mission of seeking and rescuing lost people, His blessing will be on us and fruit will happen! Then the question will be: Who is the most excited . . . the people who met Christ or the people who helped them meet Christ?

Jesus, help us to be Your light to the world around us.

So, shine Christ's light!

THINK ABOUT IT . . .

1. Who would the Lord specifically have you pray for?
2. How can you express care for each of those people?

Chapter 6

LIVE A PRAY-CARE-SHARE-LIFESTYLE

—w—

In one city, I was mentoring the pastors and preparing them to launch a citywide pray-care-share effort together on a given Sunday. I suggested they share Christ's teaching about "Love your neighbor as yourself" (Mark 12:31), then invite their people to commit to pray regularly for others they care about who need to know Christ. One pastor came to me and said, "I just can't do that. How can I ask others to love their neighbors? I have a neighbor who passed away two weeks ago. He'd been my neighbor for seven years and I don't think I had even met him or knew his name. How can I invite my congregation to love their neighbors when I am not doing it?"

"I have a suggestion for you," I said. "Go to your congregation as broken and humble about it as you are with me and tell them what you just told me. Ask them to pray with you to become a loving neighbor, and not so busy leading the church that you don't personally show interest in and care for your neighbors. People may not remember the sermon you give Sunday morning, but they'll never forget your humility and brokenness when you asked them to pray for you."

He took this advice. He also invited his congregation to start praying for others by name. He led them in this challenge: he made a list of some neighbors even though he didn't know their names—the guy three doors down; the young couple across the street, etc. Within two weeks he came back with wonderful stories about two of the neighbors he had started praying for. One of the neighbors came to his garage. They talked together and the pastor bought a golf club from him. He had a long chat with his other neighbor, and they became friends. What a strange coincidence! I encouraged him to tell the people of his church what had happened, and to thank them for praying for him to be a better neighbor. In short, the pastor became a living illustration of what happens when we focus on people, pray for them, and have others join us in prayer.

Be an Example

Begin to intentionally live a pray-care-share lifestyle and encourage others to do the same. Share who you're praying for and ask your family or small group to pray that God will help you find ways to show that you care. Be open to sharing your challenges, your fears, your doubts, your efforts, your failures, and your joys.

We live in a culture where people long to have someone who models life for them. People are screaming from their hurts, "Don't just tell me. Show me." That goes for Christians and pre-Christians. As you pray for people regularly by name,

B egin to intentionally live a pray-care-share life-style and encourage others to do the same.

find ways to show that you care, and in time they'll be interested to know why—that's the time to share something about your faith.

I believe the western style of "doing church" is much more tell than show. In the next chapter, Paul told the people of Thessalonica, "We loved you so much that we were delighted to share with you not only the gospel of God but our lives as well, because you had become so dear to us" (2:8).

Our calling is much more than sharing the good news of God with people. It's sharing our lives with them. And, it's loving them.

Early on as a pastor I learned to share my challenges honestly and openly. I remember confessing to my congregation that I'd stopped praying regularly for my brother, Bill. I had prayed for him for 20 years but didn't see much happen. People thanked me for telling them that and for being so honest, saying they had done the same. I asked them to start praying with me for him.

Later, my brother's conversion happened unexpectedly. It was a Good Friday morning when I called him to just wish him a good Easter weekend.

He said to me, "I wish some things in my life had been different. I guess it's a little late for me to be thinking about it now."

I realized that my brother's statement was God's open door, and we had a conversation about it never being too late to recognize what Jesus did on Good Friday and ask Him to forgive us for our sins.

I said, "How about just doing that now?"

He said, "Well, yeah. Why not?"

Suddenly I realized that I was praying with my brother to allow Christ to forgive his sins and for Him to be in charge of his life. I hung up the phone so excited, so stunned, so in awe of God, so surprised by my brother's openness, so amazed that the brother I actually had quit praying for had just met Christ.

Wow, did that change Easter for me! On Easter Sunday morning I concluded the services by sharing the story of my brother coming to Christ on Good Friday. And I thanked the people who had prayed with me for him. I invited other people who thought that they'd never make that commitment to Christ, to just do it. And many did—many met Christ.

So I called my brother on Monday morning and said, "Lots of people met Jesus yesterday because of you, Bill."

He said, "What &#@$& are you talking about?"

I told him that I had shared his story and that it helped others come to Christ. But it did more than that—it helped other people in the congregation to have new hope about family members who needed to know Christ. And it encouraged them to be open to the unexpected moment to naturally invite someone to know Christ.

Then the fun began. I talked to my brother week by week about the Bible. He had never read the Bible in his life, and now he was reading it and sharing his frustrations about not understanding what it said or what it meant. He was feeling guilty because he was still doing things he thought he shouldn't be doing. I watched him, a frustrated newborn in Christ, start to see things through God's eyes.

One day my brother said, "If you're coming back this summer, how about baptizing me in our sister's swimming pool?" *Where did that come from?* "Well, I just thought I should be baptized."

It happened, and his baptism impacted my whole family. But it also impacted me personally, and the church, because I openly shared with them the story of his journey. Start praying for people by name, and never give up.

I was with another pastor on a Sunday morning two weeks after he had asked his people to start praying for people by name.

"You won't believe what happened," he said. "I wrote down my brother's name and started praying consistently for him. We live in the same town but have had a broken relationship. I haven't been in his home or he in mine for 20 years. I put his name on a prayer wall in our church along with lots of other people, so we could pray for each other's friends and relatives. Would you believe my brother called me this week and said, 'Let's have dinner Saturday night.' He invited us over saying. 'It's about time we get together.'"

This pastor's heart came alive with new passion and faith.

Share with others what God is doing in your pray-care-share journey.

On Sunday morning he talked to his church in a fresh way about being focused on helping others come to Christ. Why? Because he was experiencing it. Because he was living it. Because he was seeing the power of answered prayer with his own brother. I told him, "I hope the day will come when you and your brother can tell this story together before the congregation and it will be unforgettable for everyone.

Perhaps it will be a life-changing moment for the entire congregation."

Share with others what God is doing in your pray-care-share journey. Hearing about your journey will encourage them to take the journey as well. I'm committed to loving my neighbors not because I'm a pastor but because I'm a follower of Christ.

Who Is My Neighbor?

Once, I saw a large unmarked truck backed up to a neighbor's house, with men loading or unloading something through the garage. I went over and inquired, and the men said they were just delivering a washing machine. I didn't believe it, so I got their license plate number and tried to contact our neighbors, who were out of town. I even took a picture of the truck.

Fortunately, their story turned out to be true—they were actually delivering a washing machine from a department store. But when the neighbors found out that I had been seeking to be sure their house

God opens doors of opportunity if we're looking and asking Him, "How can I serve my neighbor?"

was safe and that everything was in order, it opened a wonderful door of communication with them. They invited us to have dinner with them, and during dinner we discovered that their son-in-law had been diagnosed with aggressive cancer a few years before. In time, he came to Calvary and to Christ, and the church was a huge help to him.

It is interesting how **God opens doors of opportunity if we're looking and asking Him, "How can I serve my neighbor?"**

On another occasion I was able to love my neighbor by painting his fence. I was having my back fence painted and realized that his fence was in worse shape than mine. I felt led to have his fence painted too. He was elderly and in poor health, and he ended up in the hospital and graduated to heaven. My neighbor never got to see his painted fence. But I knew that I had done what God wanted me to do—I had responded to Christ's command to love my neighbor as I loved myself. Now, when I look on my patio and see my neighbor's fence, it's a reminder to find practical ways to care about my neighbors.

When Jesus was asked, "Which is the greatest commandment in the Law?" (Matthew 22:36), His reply was, "Love the Lord your God with all your heart and with all your soul and with all your mind." Then he added, "And . . . 'Love your neighbor as yourself'" (vv. 37,39).

Religious leaders asked Jesus, "And who is my neighbor?" In Luke 10:29, Jesus gave a surprising response in the wonderful story of the Good Samaritan. In this story, pious people had walked by the path of a man who had been robbed and injured, completely ignoring him. It was the Samaritan who stopped to help the man (see vv. 30-37).

What was Christ's point?

There are people whose paths we cross as we go about our day—people we don't expect to see; people we may not even know. These **people need our help, and we need to be ready to pray for them, care for them, and bring hope to them.**

One summer, God brought a mechanic across my path. I hired him to do some work for me and learned that his name was Nathan. I asked him where his name came from. He said he had a Jehovah's Witness background as a family and all the kids had Bible names. I shared with him that just before he arrived I was reading Scriptures about Nathan. I told him that Nathan was a man of great courage who did the right thing. I asked him, "Do you have a desire to live with courage like Nathan did?"

> *People need our help, and we need to be ready to pray for them, care for them, and bring hope to them.*

Nathan was surprised by my question. He replied, "Well, I'm not involved in the church anymore."

I said, "Well, I guess the most important thing is not whether you're involved in that church anymore, but whether you still believe that Jesus came to be your Savior." We had a conversation about it and left it there. Living a pray-care-share lifestyle is sometimes just being available to talk to people whenever, wherever, and however seems appropriate.

Last year while vacationing at Catalina Island, Beccy and I walked into a restaurant where we met a young couple. During a brief conversation we learned that the young man had just returned from his third one-year tour of duty in Iraq. They had a baby who was one and a half years old, who he'd not seen for a year. They were celebrating their third wedding anniversary. We sat at our table, feeling so grateful for this young man and for those who give their lives in military service. We instinctively knew that we needed to serve them and express gratitude to them. We looked at each other and asked, "What does God want us to do?"

We both knew.

While they were still eating I slipped out and went to a nice restaurant next door and talked to the manager. I told him about the young couple we had met and about the situation. I said, "We feel like we want to provide them with a really nice anniversary dinner tonight. Can you help?"

He enthusiastically said, "Of course. I will serve them myself, treat them royally, and fix a very special anniversary dessert for them."

I returned to where the couple was eating lunch and asked them if they had plans for that evening, and they did not. I got the impression they didn't have the resources to do much that was very special—it was special enough just being away together.

I walked outside the restaurant with them, and would you believe it, as I said, "It's your third anniversary . . . ," three WWII fighter airplanes appeared. They flew over in formation and circled where we were, then flew away. The couple stared in disbelief and felt it was a sign in the heavens of God blessing their third anniversary. Then I told them their anniversary dinner was all set for them at the restaurant on the corner. That night they had a wonderful anniversary dinner, which I think they'll remember for the rest of their lives.

The next day, I thought about some books I had brought with me, which had daily readings to encourage marriages. I went and got one of the books and brought it back to them and said, "This might be helpful to you. It has some daily

> *When you feel led by God to bless somebody and pray that they'll find hope, just do it.*

thoughts about how to maximize your marriage." I told them we just wanted to pray that God would bless their future and keep them safe and give them some great years in their marriage. I kept asking myself, *Am I being too pushy? Are we going too far?*

Let me urge you . . . ***when you feel led by God to bless somebody and pray that they'll find hope, just do it.***

I look back on that experience and realize that that was the best thing that happened all summer. It is true, it's better to give than to receive. Be ready to bless and encourage people and give them hope in any way that it works. I didn't know if I would ever hear from that young couple again, but I prayed that the book would help them both come to a strong faith in Christ.

About ten months later I received a phone call from the husband. It caught me by surprise. He said, "Thank you for the anniversary dinner. And thank you for that book—we've been reading it and talking about it. It's made a difference in our marriage." This was a confirmation—reach out and care when God encourages us to do so. We may not know the results for months, or until eternity comes.

Living a pray-care-share lifestyle is not so much about who has the gift of evangelism; it's not about how much you know the Bible; it's not about how well you can articulate your beliefs. It's simply being intentional to pray for people you love and for those Christ brings across your path. Then find ways to care . . . sometimes it's just sharing a few words, or a book, or an invitation to an event, or maybe it's something about your personal faith.

Taking this pray-care-share journey is an incredible adventure. It will change the way you look at people all around you. And, most importantly, it's identifying with Christ and His mission.

THINK ABOUT IT . . .

1. What would need to change for you to live this pray-care-share lifestyle?

2. What are ways you can put it into action? Be specific.

3. How would that affect the way you look at your day-to-day life?

Chapter 7

JUST DO IT!

—〰—

In healthy vineyards, grapes happen.

In a healthy flock of sheep, lambs happen.

In a field of healthy crops, harvest happens.

When a vine grower tends his vineyard or a shepherd cares for his sheep or a farmer cultivates his crops, they have the end in mind: The grapes, the new lambs, the harvest are the joy. The Bible talks about the joy of harvest: "Those who sow in tears will reap with songs of joy. He who goes out weeping, carrying seed to sow, will return with songs of joy, carrying sheaves with him" (Psalm 126:5-6).

In Christ's family, the great joy and excitement is seeing new birth. In healthy Christian families, new believers happen.

What percentage of people have the physical capacity to reproduce? Most, who are healthy and mature. What percentage of Christ followers have the capacity to reproduce their spiritual life in others? All who are healthy and mature.

Reproducing our life in Christ is taking Christ's final commission personally: "Therefore go and make disciples of all people" (Matthew 28:19). Healthy DNA reproduces itself. *It's natural for healthy believers to be fruitful and multiply.* When a pray-care-share lifestyle becomes natural, we change. There is new joy, new release, new life. The environment is different in a very healthy way.

When Beccy and I were at Call2All in Hong Kong, a global conference on world evangelism, I was amazed to see that many of the third-world Christians "get" it. When people meet Christ, they're encouraged within a few months to bring others together, tell them their story and invite them to follow Christ too. As a result, the Church multiplies itself within a matter of months. It's viral—healthy followers of Christ producing more followers of Christ.

> *It's natural for healthy believers to be fruitful and multiply.*

Let me walk through some very practical principles to help us develop this healthy pray-care-share DNA.

1. **It's inclusive not exclusive.** Can every believer pray for people God puts on their heart? Can every believer look for ways to serve and care? Can every believer share a word, a smile or a personal story when the time is right about how

Christ touched and changed their life? The answer, of course, is a resounding, YES!

Through the guidance of the Holy Spirit *you* can do it! It can be totally normal. As you become intentional about living a pray-care-share lifestyle you will stop thinking, *I'm scared of evangelism. I don't know enough. I don't know if I'll say the right thing.* When you take a step of faith and start to live a pray-care-share lifestyle you will discover an amazing fact, and will say:

> *When prayer moves to action, it's amazing what happens!*

"I *can* do this! I *am* doing it!"

2. **It's exponential.** When you pray for somebody for a while, and then ask God to show you a way to care for that person, what happens? The impact of your prayers is multiplied exponentially. Prayer is primary. Prayer is essential. And . . . **when prayer moves to action, it's amazing what happens!** Let me give you some illustrations of this concept.

My assistant shared with me that she had a Jewish friend who lived a distance away. She had been praying for this woman for a long time, but the woman was just not open to Christianity. So, my assistant—who is quite indoctrinated with this stuff now—said, "My friend called me the other day and is all upset." The friend said, "I lost my beloved little dog. I'm going to put out notices in the neighborhood and try to see if we can find my dog." My assistant drove an hour and a half to her friend's house and helped distribute the flyers around the neighborhood. Why did she do this for her friend? It was a way to serve and show love to her. The woman couldn't believe it. It softened her heart to know that somebody would care enough to drive that far to help her find her lost dog. My assistant's simple act, moving from praying for this friend to doing something to show care for her, was powerful in opening the relationship.

It's exponential. Prayer + care = exponential impact.

3. **It's sequential.** Intercessory prayer—leads to care—and opens the door to share. There's a great difference between praying for people to know Christ in general and praying for specific people by name. I've observed many individuals and small groups where people are praying for others to know Christ, using "no-name, vanilla prayers." I've observed so few who are praying for specific people by name.

I encourage you not to be uptight about sharing. Just pray for people and let relationships develop naturally. God will show you when it's right, and the right way to share. Just keep praying that they'll find Christ's forgiveness and hope. Sometimes God will even bring this about without your sharing a word.

I started praying for a new neighbor who recently had a stroke that left him physically unattractive. As a result, few people spoke to him. I made it a point to strike up a conversation with him occasionally. One day I asked him about his career and he told me he had helped develop a master plan and launch a major food corporation in America, Trader Joe's. I occasionally asked him questions about leadership—how he developed staff, how he developed a strategy, how he determined the market locations, etc. I learned that he was teaching in the business school at UCLA, and I found that as we talked, I was learning principles about leadership from him.

One day he said to me, "This is an unfriendly neighborhood. You're my best friend since I moved here."

You see, when I moved from praying for my neighbor to starting to show interest in him, things changed *exponentially*.

The day came when I saw him in a restaurant. He said, "I am having surgery again this week."

I sat down to talk with him briefly and asked, "How are you feeling about your surgery tomorrow?" After he told me, I asked, "Have you thought about just trusting God with tomorrow's surgery and with your future?"

The opportunity was so natural. One minute later I joined him in praying to trust God with the coming surgery and with all of his life. I left the table four minutes later and felt like that was God's time and way to share. It started with praying; then finding ways to care; then seeing the right opportunity to share personally about trusting Christ. Praying plus caring multiplies the impact and influence and opens doors for sharing.

4. **It's celebration.** With your family and friends, do you celebrate when a new child is born? Of course. When your family, friends, or neighbors discover life and hope in Christ, it's time to celebrate. Celebrate the good news!

A pastor in one of the churches I coached said to me, "In our church we have roses to celebrate the birth of new babies. We also have white roses to celebrate people who have come to Christ in the past week. Every Sunday, as people walk in to our church, they eagerly look to see if there are any new white roses."

The point is: Find ways to celebrate the new life God is bringing, to help people be aware of all that God is doing to bring new life.

Luke 15 tells the parables of the lost coin and the lost son. The lost coin represented part of a woman's wedding band, which women in the Middle East cultures wear— bands with coins around their heads. These are like a

> *All of heaven rejoices when people who have lost their way find Christ. So should we!*

dowry, part of the gift given to them at the time of their marriage. The joy over the lost coin is not like the joy in finding a quarter, it's the joy of finding your lost wedding ring.

The prodigal son is a universal story. Many families have a child who in his childhood, adolescence, or adulthood loses his way. The concern is overwhelming and heartbreaking for parents. There is no greater joy than when that child returns.

These stories have that same common factor—the joy of finding what was lost. *All of heaven rejoices when people who have lost their way find Christ. So should we!*

An older lady had not seen her son for seven years. She was estranged from him and had no idea where he was. When her church started praying for people by name, this lady wrote her son's name on a bookmark. She asked the people in her small group to pray with her for her son. Within two weeks she received a long letter from her son explaining that he had met Jesus and was sorry for the broken relationship and hoped to come and be restored to his mom again. She told her group, and they cried and praised God together.

I encouraged the pastor to have her share her story on Sunday with the whole congregation—to let them in on the joy of her son coming to Christ and coming back home! She did share her story, and it had an incredible impact on the congregation. It helped people refocus on others who needed Christ. It reaffirmed that by praying together, amazing things can happen. It caused those who heard the story to think about the prodigal, or lost, person in their lives and infused them with faith to believe.

5. **Keep it visual.** Write the names of people you're praying for in some place and in some way where it becomes a *keeper* for you. This is not a to-do list for a week; this is a prayer list for the rest of your life.

At Calvary Community, I encouraged people to develop a pray-care-share lifestyle. One of the visual tools we used were bookmarks. They were intended to be kept in the people's Bibles or with them for a long time. The bookmark included a line or two about the meaning of praying-caring-sharing, and provided a place where people could write the names of those they would pray for regularly: family; friends; neighbors; work associates; schoolmates.

Another tool we used was a lighthouse wall. Let me tell you how God brought that about. James Coleman, who is a world-class artist—you'll see his paintings in studios all over the world—came to my son, Kirk, and said, "Thank you for how much this church has done to help my kids. I want to paint a painting for your dad and the church."

My son said, "Well, why don't you paint a lighthouse, because that's what my dad's into right now. We're talking about everyone being a lighthouse for Christ."

But James said, "No, no. I don't paint lighthouses. I paint scenes."

A few weeks later I got a call from Kirk, saying that we needed to go over to James Coleman's studio. So we went to the studio, walked in, and there on the wall was a five-by-five-foot painting of a lighthouse. I was immediately drawn to it.

"That's yours," James said. "Thanks for your influence in my family. Do anything you want with it."

I asked, "Could I make prints of it?"

He answered, "Whatever you want. If you want lithographs of it, do it. It's yours. It's my gift and thank-you for what you did for my kids."

I didn't know but found out later that that painting was valued at several thousand dollars. It has been mounted in our church lobby, well secured to a high wall. The day we revealed the painting to our congregation, James came and talked about painting it. And do you know what happened to him? He started coming to church—even sitting in the front. His life started to change.

"You know what?" he said. "By painting that lighthouse for you—which I initially did not want to do—I've become a lighthouse for Christ. From now on, I'm going to put John 8:12—'I am the light of the world'—on every painting I paint. I realize this may kill my career—it may be over. But I'm going to put that Scripture on every painting."

About a year later I asked James how that Scripture was impacting his career. He answered, "You know what? God has blessed my career, rather than it destroying it."

That lighthouse painting became a tool that God used in the congregation to give us a visual reminder of who we are in Christ and of our partnership in His mission.

James later painted a replica of the lighthouse on an extended wall, 36 feet long by 8 feet high. During church services, I asked people to walk to the wall and write on it, first names only, of people they were praying for to know Christ. The caveat was that I asked them to not put a name on the wall unless they had first put it on their bookmark and had committed to pray for and care about that person. **Within a matter of weeks we had more than 20,000 names on that wall.**

During Sunday services, I would frequently ask people to walk over to the wall, or look at it, or pull out their bookmarks, and together we would pray for the names of the people on the wall or bookmarks. On Sunday morning I frequently took time to pray during the service for names that might be on that wall. Sometimes this was only a minute. I did it for the sake of the people whose names were on the wall, but I also did it to develop a culture in the congregation so that they would persevere in prayer for others.

I've had the opportunity to work with pastors and leaders in 20+ cities across the nation, and they are now leading and encouraging people in their churches to live a pray-care-share lifestyle. One pastor friend in Chicago decided to use the Bible, rather than a bookmark, as a visual reminder for his people to pray, care, and share. On Sunday he turned to the book of Revelation and read these passages: "Anyone whose name was not found written in the book of life was thrown into the lake of fire" (20:15), and "Nothing impure will ever enter it, nor will anyone who does what is shameful or deceitful, but only those whose names are written in the Lamb's book of life" (21:27). Then he asked the people to open their Bibles to the back, where there's a blank page after the book of Revelation, and write the names of those they were going to pray for—that those people would have their names written in the Lamb's book of life. Powerful!

It Works!

In Treasure Valley, Idaho, the churches scheduled a pray-care-share event over Labor Day weekend and they called the event "Labor of Love." Together the church members did a makeover at the high school in the center of town, improving the landscaping, painting, and repairing windows. They prepared the school for a fresh opening for the fall semester. The local newspaper and television captured the story and pictures and publicized how the churches served together to meet a critical need in their community.

Imagine one city in Iowa, where 37 churches decided to refocus their congregations on a lifestyle of pray-care-share. On one specific Sunday, all of the churches gave out pray-care-share bookmarks to the people who were present and asked them to identify people they would pray for. They wrote down these names on their bookmarks. On that one given Sunday there were three or four hundred followers of Christ in those churches who wrote four to eight names on their bookmarks of people they would start praying for. Can you imagine the spiritual impact the Body of Christ had on that city? Can you imagine five or six thousand believers, each praying for six people—that's 36,000 people by name being prayed for daily to know Christ! The city was Cedar Rapids. They even called their effort "Serve the City."

Later, major floods hit the Midwest, and the most catastrophic area was in Cedar Rapids. As the waters rose, the police and fire departments were maxed out. People from these very churches began going door to door to hundreds of homes to assist people. Church leaders opened the doors of their churches and provided shelter to many. Their prayers led to an incredible opportunity to care for and profoundly impact their city.

Coachella Valley, California, was another community to adopt an areawide pray-care-share effort. I was privileged to come alongside Paul Cedar, president of Mission America, and the pastors of the city to develop LOV—Love the Valley. After a few years, the pastors and churches of the cities in Coachella Valley came together for a Festival of Life. The numbers of people attending the festival and being prayed for, cared for, and shared with were astounding: 56,500 people participated in the festival events; thousands received free eye exams and glasses, free dental services and general medical care; 20,000 food boxes were distributed; and 3,600 people made personal commitments to turn their lives over to Christ.

Another amazing care project was developed in Calvary Community Church. Some leaders felt led to adopt a city 25 miles away, in Piru, California, where life was very modest and the people lived on the edge of poverty. We targeted a day of service, and 500 volunteers from one city traveled 25 miles to another to work side-by-side with the residents to give a facelift to several blocks of their town. Opportunities were available for everyone—adults, youth, children—to be involved in the "extreme town makeover," improving neighborhood parkways, general cleanup, weed abatement, fence repair, painting, gardening, electrical work, even hauling away cars or other junked items.

It was an amazing experience to later drive down the main street and see the facelift of the downtown community. It gave an incredible boost to the spirits of the residents and a fresh pride in their town; and it built a bridge between two very different communities of people—all in the name of Christ. It transformed not only the main street of Piru, but hearts of people in that community and of the volunteers from Calvary Community Church as well.

When you start praying for people by name, expect things to happen!

Whatever you come up with, have a written list of specific names of who you're praying for. Put it in your Bible, on your mirror, somewhere. **Powerful things happen when we write down names of people and are reminded to pray consistently for them.**

6. **Tell the stories.** Remember the old gospel song, "I Love to Tell the Story of Jesus and His Love"? Jesus told stories—He loved to tell stories. So, tell your stories. Share your fears about reaching

> *Powerful things happen when we write down names of people and are reminded to pray consistently for them.*

out to your neighbor and share your challenges. Also share the joys of the good things God does. When people leave church on Sunday mornings, which would they remember more, the teaching, or a story of someone who reached out to a neighbor in love and something happened for Christ?

When Acts 2:42 talks about the early church of Jerusalem, it says that they devoted themselves to teaching, yes, but also to fellowship. I think fellowship means the sharing of what God was doing in their lives and what was happening in their lives. They shared stories when they came together on the Lord's day. What has a greater impact on people than stories—real, life stories? As pastor I made sure that part of our service was devoted to having people share stories of what God was doing in their lives.

One very fun Sunday-morning, a 10-year-old boy who had just met Christ was being baptized. He said, "I asked Jesus to come in to my life because my sister did—and she became a whole lot nicer to me after that." A lot of laughter followed, but people heard a profound message about Christ affecting our attitudes.

After a teaching at Calvary about loving our enemies, a couple who were new in Christ felt convicted to love their ex-spouses. Some time later, at a Sunday-morning service, I walked over to this couple and, with their permission, interviewed them about their recent experience. They shared their story with the congregation.

"I felt led to go to my ex-wife and her new husband and invite them to know Christ, too. They came to church, and met Him." Can you imagine the Sunday when these couples were baptized together? No sermon will impact people's hearts as powerfully as this living illustration did.

Wonderful personal stories help people to see the power of God to change lives, and to encourage them that they too can love and pray for others to know Christ.

7. **Have celebration events**. Have a pool party in your backyard or a dinner party together with friends or an event at church—just find ways to celebrate and congratulate people who have found new life and hope in Christ.

We always had a New Life Sunday in January, when we asked who had found Christ as the light of their life in the past year. I would offer some scriptural thought about new life or a new hope in Christ, and then say, "Who found Christ's light this last year? I'd like to congratulate you on beginning a new year with Christ in your life." There was always a scary moment for me, wondering what would happen. Then bit by bit, people would indicate they had met Christ. I'd walk out to them and talk with them about what happened and who helped them find Christ and how it happened. It became an incredible celebration of new life.

Some people said that was the most important Sunday of the year for them.

When we first started our annual celebration of new life, a man walked up to me after a service and asked, "Could I bring some bushels of apples next week? Could we just pass out apples to celebrate the fruit, the harvest?" From that next Sunday on, we had an annual Apple Sunday at Calvary. We gave apple pins to everybody who acknowledged in January that they had met Christ the previous year, and we gave apple pins to the people who helped them come to

Christ. As people continued to wear the apple pins, the pins became a point of interest and friends and family would ask, "What's the apple pin about?" And they would tell them.

On Apple Sundays we not only passed out apple pins, but apples—bushels of apples, at the end of the service. I would ask everyone to take an apple, hold it, and pray that God would bring fruit from their life in the coming year. We prayed that they would plant seeds in other people's lives. We closed the services with everyone taking a bite out of their apple. It was tasty, refreshing, wonderful—but not nearly as refreshing and wonderful as the fruit God would bring the next year. This event created an exciting culture in the church where healthy fruit was expected. People left, anticipating the harvest through their prayer, care, and sharing.

It's doubtful anyone could forget the young man who stood up in church and shared his story with the congregation.

"I met Christ because I found out my mom was fasting and praying for me to have a change in my life and to know Christ. I came to Christ because I was scared of what was going to happen to my mom, because she was fasting and not eating."

Stories like these are so impactful and transformational that everyone understands we can all pray and care and share Christ with others.

Baptism became a celebration event at Calvary Community—especially when people were baptized by the person who had helped them come to Christ. That was a huge change for our congregation, and baptisms became a joyous time for the participants and the observers.

Everyone who was there remembers the day when an articulate businesswoman stood up in church and said, "I was an atheist . . . I was not into religious things at all. But Susan has been my secretary for these many years, and as I watched her faith in Christ I became more and more impressed, and I decided I needed the faith she had. She helped me believe in Jesus. And today's she's going to baptize me."

In the church you attend, what if people were baptized by the person who helped them come to Christ? Can you imagine that? What would that say about pray-care-share being a part of the normal culture of your church? What would it say about the joy of new life? What would it say about empowering people or trusting people? What would it say to those observing, and wondering if they could be a witness to their neighbors?

The impact of people baptizing others and the congregation hearing their stories is as powerful as any sermon you'll ever hear.

At Calvary Community, it was all about creating an environment where reproduction was normal; people felt welcomed; joy was expressed; the church body was engaged and fruit happened. It's powerful when church gatherings become times of . . .

- celebration
- sharing what God is doing in the Body
- telling exciting stories about new spiritual births
- expressing the same joy we'll have in heaven
- encouraging others to believe.

Every follower of Christ can be engaged in a lifestyle of praying for people around us to have hope in Christ, of finding ways to care and show love and listen, and of sharing when we know the time is right, in a way that's appropriate. Let pray-care-share become the core of a fresh DNA in your spiritual life. Just as everything God produces has life and the capacity to reproduce itself, the believers and our churches themselves become places where healthy reproduction is normal.

THINK ABOUT IT . . .

1. What visual reminders can you use to encourage you to pray for specific people by name?

2. Can you describe instances where you began to care for someone and your relationship changed?

3. How can you encourage others to share their stories about coming to Christ or helping bring someone to Him?

4. What are your greatest fears about sharing Christ with others?

Chapter 8

LIVE READY—CHRIST IS COMING

—ɯ—

One Sunday, as people entered church, each received a beautifully designed wedding invitation that read:

The Father requests your presence

at the wedding banquet of His Son, Jesus Christ,

Who gave His life—in loving sacrifice—for you.

This glad and glorious event

will be held in heaven;

Date and time to be announced when He returns.

Please RSVP immediately

Only those who have responded to His

loving invitation will be admitted.

As the people entered the church that day, they saw a very long, elegant banquet table set with fine china, crystal, silver, and floral arrangements. The banquet table took up the full length of the center aisle.

That coming banquet is described in the book of Revelation: "For the wedding of the Lamb has come, and his bride has made herself ready. Blessed are those who are invited to the wedding supper of the Lamb!" (vv. 7,9).

Have you tried to imagine what that day will be like?

At Christ's farewell dinner with the disciples, He said, "Do this in remembrance of me" (Luke 22:19). The Lord's Supper is really a way for us to look back and remember that Christ gave His life for us. But it's also about looking forward to sitting at the banquet table with Him in heaven. At that farewell dinner, Christ said to His disciples, "I tell you, I will not drink again of the fruit of the vine until the kingdom of God comes" (v. 18). He was envisioning the day when they would be literally in the presence of Christ in heaven.

After teaching this wonderful prophecy from Revelation, I invited people to come to the wedding table, on which were placed bread and wine for Communion. First, I invited those people who had never before accepted the invitation from Christ. Several came to the banquet table, accepting the invitation and declaring their new faith in Christ. They had their first Communion! Then, I invited everyone to come—those who had previously accepted Christ's invitation. People left that morning with an unforgettable impression of the glorious reunion we will have with Christ someday.

How often is the big day mentioned in services at the church you attend? How often do you and other believers talk about it? That's really the Big Day. That's the great hope.

On another occasion, our church service began with a loud, vibrant wedding march. I stood and invited everyone to stand. A beautifully dressed bride—veiled so no one could recognize the individual—walked down the aisle and up onto the platform. She knelt at the foot of a cross. I'm not sure how many words or thoughts from my sermon were remembered by people that morning. But they did catch the significance of living a pure life, being ready and anticipating the day when, as part of Christ's Bride, they will kneel before Him . . . welcomed into eternity.

Have you spoken to a young lady about to be married? The most obvious question she is asked is, "When's the big day?" Her reply to that question will never be, "What big day?" She *knows* what big day. She's preoccupied with it; it's the focus of her attention, passion, and hope. She's eagerly looking forward to it and can hardly wait for that day.

As a guy, it's a bit harder to imagine myself as a part of Christ's *Bride*. But I can connect with a bride's loyalty and focus on her groom, and immersing herself in him. The main thing for me personally is that I love and am devoted to Jesus Christ, with all of my heart and all of my energy, staying focused on my relationship with Him.

Beccy and I had planned a trip to Hawaii. We had prepared well; made plane reservations early; talked about where we would go and what we'd like to do. We had made reservations where we

> *When Christ comes back, the only thing that will really matter is: Who's ready?*

would stay. We had bought some new clothes; packed carefully, and repacked. We had done everything we could do to prepare for this wonderful, romantic trip and we were very excited about it. We had scheduled a van to pick us up at 4:00 in the morning to get to LAX in time for a very early flight.

When we went to bed I set the alarm; we went to sleep, and the next thing I remember is Beccy waking me up and asking, "Do you hear someone knocking at our front door?" Her next question was, "What time is it?" I looked at the clock and, sure enough, it was about 4:00 a.m.—the time we were supposed to be picked up.

She asked, "Didn't you set the alarm?"

"Of course I set the alarm!" Then I realized I had set it, but I hadn't pulled the lever to activate it.

I rushed downstairs to answer the door and it was the van driver. I said, "Could you please wait—even 15 minutes?"

He said, "No, I've got other people in the van and must go."

So we went into panic mode. We decided our only option was to drive ourselves to the airport. We hurried but were late getting to LAX. We were tense—I was *very* tense. We ran to the gate and nearly missed the flight. But we made it.

All we had done to prepare, all of our plans and dreams, seemed unimportant—*all that mattered was making that flight.*

Do you know what I was thinking about during the flight to our paradise vacation? My mind was on the journey

> *Who do you know who needs to get ready?*

that followers of Christ will make the day He comes back for His Bride. I thought about the many things that occupy our time and interests—so much to do, so much to finish. I realized that **when Christ comes back, the only thing that will really matter is: Who's ready?** All we've been talking about in this book so far has been focusing on Christ and His mission. Our ultimate destination is being with Christ forever. In a sense, all of life is planning and preparing for the final, ultimate journey.

Christ's mission and our work is to prepare people to make the flight. ***Who do you know who needs to get ready?***

Pray for them right now.

Ask how you can serve and show Christ's love to them.

Pray that you'll be God's instrument to help them find Christ, as God opens the doors.

The vision statement I used at Calvary was, "To help as many people as possible to be ready for Christ's return." When church people get beyond themselves and stop asking what's in it for them, and focus on praying and serving people who need to know Christ, the church will be transformed.

As I've spoken with pastors and Christian leaders in cities across the nation, I've asked, "How many of you really believe that Jesus Christ is coming back to earth someday?" Of course, everybody raises their hand. Then I've followed with the question: ***Did you get up today and say to yourself, "This could be the day!"?*** Rarely have I seen a pastor's hand go up when asked this question. And their response pointed me to the obvious conclusion: "Well, I guess we all believe that Jesus Christ is coming back but we don't really expect it. At least not today."

In Christ's final warnings to his disciples before He went to the cross, He spoke specifically about his return. "Keep watch, because you do not know on what day your Lord will come" (Matthew 24:42). I've often said to a roomful of pastors,

Did you get up today and say to yourself, "This could be the day!"?

90

"Matthew 24 must be talking about us—we all believe He's coming, but nobody expects Him today!"

Later, when Christ was talking about some virgins being ready for the groom to come, He said: "Keep watch, because you do not know the day or the hour" (Matthew 25:13). Some of the virgins were ready, while some had to run out to get more oil for their lamps and missed Him. Part of the vitality of a healthy Christ follower is living ready to meet Christ . . . living with expectations that He's coming back again.

Focus on the day when Christ comes. Not only is this part of our theology, but it must be part of our focus and of our worship *every day!*

So, when is the big day of Christ's coming? We don't know the day or the hour. But we'd better live ready. That's His challenge, and that's what was on His mind as He taught the principles of Matthew 24 and 25.

Here's a summary:

"No one knows the day or the hour" (24:36).

"Watch" (v. 42).

"Be ready" (v. 44).

"Keep watch" (25:13).

"Well done, good and faithful servant" (25:23).

Jesus obviously wanted to make the point: Live ready, because I'm coming when you don't expect it.

If Christ's coming is our focus, how will it affect our thinking, our behavior, our days, our relationships? *If Christ's coming is on my mind, I will be thinking about family and friends who need Christ*'s help and may not be ready to meet Him. *This doesn't make us more judgmental; it makes us more caring, sensitive, and prayerful.* We will be looking for ways to serve people and show that we care. We will be open for an opportunity to share Christ.

With this focus much will happen:

- Believers' lives and attitudes will change.

- Our serve will improve.

- Our heart for people will increase.

- We will start living beyond ourselves.

And, most importantly: **Christ's mission and vision will come alive**. As we anticipate His return and *act like we really believe it*, we will instinctively help bring our friends, neighbors, and family to Him!

I get a knot in the pit of my stomach whenever a church service is over and the parting words are, "See you next Sunday." Instead, I have frequently encouraged people with, "Live ready! This could be the day! Maybe we'll see you next Sunday—or in heaven!"

> *If Christ's coming is on my mind, I will be thinking about family and friends who need Christ.*

Christ's coming—our focus of joy.

Think about the incredible joy we will have when Christ returns and we realize we've had influence in helping others to follow Him. If we refocus on Christ as the center of the church as well as our ultimate hope of His return, it will impact *everyone* around us.

There were two large skylights in the building we purchased for our new church home. I insisted that each skylight have a Scripture that focused on Christ's coming again. When people look up to those skylights, they read:

- "To him be glory and power for ever and ever. Amen. Look, he is coming with the clouds, and every eye will see him." (Revelation 1:6-7)

- "At that time they will see the Son of Man coming in a cloud with power and great glory." (Luke 21:27)

Why was it important to do this? Because when people walk through the building and look up toward the light, I want them to see Scripture and think about Christ's coming again.

Christ's coming—our great hope.

Outside of Vancouver on Highway 5 there are steep mountain drops and tunnels. Amidst all of the dangers, suddenly I saw a sign reading: Entering Hope. That's right, there literally is a place called Hope near Vancouver, Canada. And when I saw that sign and entered that city, I thought about helping people find the ultimate road to hope.

Got hope? People without Christ are described as people without hope. "Remember that at that time you were separate from Christ, excluded from citizenship in Israel and foreigners to the covenants of the promise, without hope and without God in the world" (Ephesians 2:12). Our challenge is to help people find faith in Christ, to live experiencing and sharing Christ's love, and to live with hope that He's coming.

One of the most powerful expressions of hope in the New Testament is Paul's benediction in Romans 15:13: "May the God of hope fill you with joy and peace as you trust in him so that you will overflow with hope by the power of the Holy Spirit." In other words, may you be "full of it"!

Hope brings with it joy.

Hope brings with it peace.

The Holy Spirit's intention is to cause us to overflow with the hope of Christ's coming again. It's life transforming.

So, do you have hope? Hope about the future? What's the hope of your life? What's the hope of the church?

Paul said, in his writing to Titus, "We wait for the blessed hope, the glorious appearing of our great God and Savior, Jesus Christ" (2:13). Christ's return—that's the great hope!

Romans 12:2 says, "Be joyful in hope."

Ephesians 1:18 says, "Know the hope to which you were called, the riches of his glorious inheritance."

Christ's coming—our motivation to live a pure life.

Jesus promised a reward, "Blessed are the pure in heart, for they will see God" (Matthew 5:8). Paul prayed for a pure life in the believers at Philippi, "That you may be able to discern what is best and may be pure and blameless until the day of Christ" (Philippians 1:10). And to the believers at Corinth, Paul wrote, "I am jealous for you with a godly jealousy. I promised you to one husband, to Christ, so that I might present you as a pure virgin to him" (2 Corinthians 11:2).

The Apostle John says, "We know that when [Christ] appears, we shall be like him, for we shall see him as he is. All who have this hope in him purify themselves, just as he is pure" (1 John 3:2-3). If I think that Jesus Christ could be coming back today, am I going to do things that morally violate Him and His Word?

Christ's coming again is the greatest motivation to live a morally pure life.

Christ's coming—our ultimate expectation.

We have a beautiful, upscale European-styled promenade mall in our community. The focal point of the mall is a dramatic and inspiring fountain designed by a renowned sculptor, De L'Esprie. It portrays a young mother reaching to the sky with excitement, holding a kite in one hand and reaching back with the other hand to her two children. Both of the children are looking up with excitement, their hands in the air. Not far away on a park bench is the dad, sitting and reading a newspaper, unaware of what is really happening.

At the commissioning of the fountain and the opening of the mall, I sat with De L'Esprie. She said, "This piece is about the coming of Christ. The mother and her children are leaving to meet Him in the sky; the dad is sitting on the bench, wondering what just happened." De L'Esprie named the sculpture "Rapture"; however, the mall management chose to rename it "Joy to Life" and put a kite in the hand of the mother. Every time I walk through that mall I'm reminded of our ultimate expectation. There it is, clearly visible before all the people of the community who walk by. Most are oblivious to its real meaning and are living without that great expectation.

In 1 Thessalonians, which is the book about Christ's coming again, Paul gives an inspiring benediction: "May your whole spirit and soul and body be kept blameless at the coming of our Lord Jesus Christ" (5:23).

I have a longing to see Christ. Do you?

At one point during the time I wrote this book, I was literally on my way to Rome. While there, I entered the Mamertine

Prison, where Paul wrote some of his last letters. I experienced this musty, stinky prison near the Roman Forum. The last book Paul wrote was 2 Timothy, and his farewell address was filled with excitement:

> There is in store for me the crown of righteousness, which the Lord, the righteous Judge, will award me on that day—and not only to me but also to all those who have longed for his appearing. (2 Timothy 4:8)

Paul had a longing to see Christ. ***I have a longing to see Christ. Do you?***

What Paul was imagining, while sitting in that prison a short distance from the coliseum and stadium, was Nero, the emperor of Rome—the leader of the world—awarding people who won a race. The crowd would roar and applaud them. Paul knew that he'd never be in that coliseum, although he could hear the roar from his prison cell. He would never be applauded or recognized by this unrighteous emperor of the world. He would never be awarded a laurel wreath crown by Nero.

But Paul had something better to look forward to. He knew that: "There is in store for me the crown of ***This could be the day!*** righteousness, which the Lord, the righteous Judge, will award to me on that day—for winning the race of life" (2 Timothy 4:8). Then Paul added,

"But it's not just for me. It's for all people who long for his appearing" (author's paraphrase).

So, are you looking forward to that day? That's the Big Day. That's really the great hope. May it become the hope and desire for every person we know and care about: that we'll learn to live ready because . . . ***This could be the day!*** May God help us all to stay focused on Christ and to be engaged in the great work of Christ—helping people to be ready for the great and glorious day of His return.

So, let's live Christ:

- Personally committed to Jesus Christ as ***Savior***;
- Actively following Jesus Christ as ***Lord***;
- Eagerly anticipating the return of Christ as ***King***.

FOR CHRIST'S SAKE, LET'S LIVE READY . . .

AND HELP AS MANY PEOPLE AS POSSIBLE TO BE READY

FOR THE GREAT AND GLORIOUS DAY OF CHRIST'S RETURN!

THIS COULD BE THE DAY!

\# \# \#

End Notes

—∿—

1. C. J. Mahaney, "The Cross-Centered Life: Keeping the Gospel the Main Thing," [http://books.google.com], accessed 13 December, 2011.

CPSIA information can be obtained at www.ICGtesting.com
Printed in the USA
BVOW042152300912

301573BV00001B/8/P